My Poetic Soul Unleashed

Melica Niccole

Hampton Publishing House, LLC

My Poetic Soul Unleashed was published by
Hampton Publishing House, LLC

P.O. Box 29201

Columbus, Ohio 43229

Copyright © 2011 by Melica Niccole

All rights reserved. This book may not be reproduced in any manner without the written consent from the publisher.

ISBN 978-0-9828745-2-3

Printed in the United States of America

Poems Written by

Melica Niccole

Edited by

Janet Slike

Book Design by

Hampton Publishing House, LLC

Publishing Company

Hampton Publishing House, LLC

Dedication

This book is dedicated to life. Though many of us will not live the same life, we will be presented with many challenges in life. These challenges will require us to act in a particular manner that has the possibility of defining who we are or who we will be. Make that defining moment count by giving life your all.

The poems below were first published on the following websites:

From Pretty Women Wonder
MelicaNiccolesRealmofCreativity.blogspot.com

Words: A Skilled Craft
MelicaNiccolesRealmofCreativity.blogspot.com
MelicaNiccole.com

Ditch Diggers
Facebook.com/people/Melica-Niccole/500553067

Includes 26 Poems

Featuring Author's Favorites

Prophet ...Pg. 2

The Womb: Life or Death...Pg. 8

Ditch Digger...Pg. 11

A Street Called Daddy...Pg. 18

This is Temporary...Pg. 27

TV Show Poetry...Pg. 36

Born to Be Deep...Pg. 42

Words: A Skilled Craft...Pg. 44

From Pretty Women Wonder...Pg. 46

Locked Gaze and Immovable Passion...Pg. 49

Love Unreciprocated...Pg. 51

Surface-Oriented People...Pg. 53

Life's Challenges and Celebratory Moments

My Life…Pg. 59

Almost Raped…Pg. 59

We Fall Down, But We Get Up…Pg. 63

Just Me!...Pg. 66

What Will Be…Pg. 68

Inspired

I'm inspired to be

What I need to be

Inspired to take a path less traveled

For this is where my world unravels

Step aside and just let me be

Because like my counterparts

I just want to be free

Prophet

I was told on April Fool's

Beware of the power of prophecy

I listened

His statement

Came like a time in Rome

When Julius Caesar was told

"Beware of the Ides of March"

Though many would have disregarded his statements

Because he was of the tattered sort

I listened

I listened because I knew within his torn spirit

Lied an unconditioned character

Who was knowledgeable about many things,

Even living the life of one without a home

One without possessions

Without a family to uplift him

And without a love to share his misfortunes with

I watched every day

As he carried the same bag

Smiled the same smile

And talked the same talk

His eyes rarely met mine

For he knew the consequences of his past indiscretions,

Which he carried so deeply in his spirit

That he would lash out at those who thought differently about him

He asked me

Does this offend people so much

That they are willing to jeopardize their place in the Kingdom of God

For a quick laugh?

I looked at his home in a bag

And and answered honestly

"Maybe"

I felt touched by his words

And at the same time hurt

Touched that his words trailed into my spirit

And left footprints on my mind

Hurt that people would treat him so negatively

And judge him as if they were free of sin

Or held an eternal pass to the Kingdom of Salvation

His spirit became so enraged at the hate-filled environment

That I had to pacify his hurt

To keep him moving toward the light

I told him that sometimes we as a people

Let people's thoughts or actions get the best of us

And act differently than how we intended to act

I told him to let it go

And be free of the same hatred that plagued his adversaries

He shook his head and knew he had to let go

However not without a few choice words before his departure

He left stating

"Remember, you draw more flies with honey than salt"

Meaning that you draw more people when you speak kind words

Than when you don't

His character is forever imprinted on my soul

Loving Me Is Easy

Loving me is easy

The hard part is letting go

But there comes a time in life

When this statement becomes so

Just be strong

And open your grasp

Because holding onto something that's not yours

Will never last

Loving me is easy

The hard part is letting go

Now it's time to say goodbye

Because it's time for me to go

Want Ad

Loyal

Reliable man who trods along

In pursuit of dreams bigger than those

Who try to link themselves to others

Because they represent continuous passion

Determined to be more than a mere

Undirected object with a destiny to fail,

While longing for ultimate fulfillment

The spirit of southern comfort

With a magnetic

Down-to-earth aura

That eases the raging spirit

He is sensual by nature

With abilities of erasing mistakes

And bringing harmony amongst others

Creation of a romantic, protective being

With artistic capabilities that bares the pain of struggle

But shows no indication of defeat

He's loving

Caring

A self-unabsorbed man

Who seeks the truth and does not ravish in lies

He who takes care of children

Though they were born

Without biological factors

However has chosen to be the inherent parent

He…

He who I speak so freely about

He..

He is the true definitive man.

The Womb: Life or Death

I was born in the womb

With enough passion to embellish my capsule

And dispense light from my mouth

Dispense a beam that only Seeing Eye dogs can see

Mimes can hear

And grandparents can smell

My purpose

I found true pleasure in exposing my well-crafted talents

That were mere possibilities

A couple of years ago

Perfected my craft

And liberated my spirit

To a magnitude immeasurable

Let's fly to the moon, Alice

I take to those words

Like an eight-year-old child takes to riding a bicycle

Without the training wheels on

Mounting the beast

Revealing beauty from the wind

Blowing through the wheels of opportunity

I thrust forward forcefully

That I have no other choice

Than to make it to the mountaintop

The journey is so chaotic

That other riders have decided to take a break

And return home

There's *No Point of Return* for me

Only visits and memories

Of how life use to be

I use those past thoughts and memories

To define my own opportunities

Because life and death lies within me

The life of my dreams

Or the death of my purpose

Which displays so definitely on the faces of mankind

Who tell me to pick one craft to master

Because I cannot do it all

I ignore those very words

Because those words

Are true for those who believe in them

I believe no such truths

Because I am more than a

Creative, boxed-in, talented, spoken, magician

I am more than a one trade

One craft

Skilled artist

I am me

And that's all I need to be

Ditch Digger

I'm digging ditches

They said a pot of gold was at the end of the rainbow

But I must have missed it

Digging for my opportunity

Because it must be buried

Waiting for me to get on my knees

Because upon its retrieval

We going to get married

Submitting ourselves to each other

Because it was love at first conversation

This isn't something to sweep under the rug

Because I will be waiting

I'm mentally attracted to you

Passionately in tune with you

Told the police

To put out an APB on you

But until we cross each other's path

I'll still be digging ditches

Looking for a pot of gold at the end of the rainbow

Because I'm bound to be with you

If I Could Freeze Time…

If I could freeze time... (dot, dot, dot)

I would

Freeze the portion in life that meant the most

The portion that gave me undeniable truth to my life

No *Imitation of Life* for me

Please

The portion that took the doubt off my shoulders

And off the faces of those that considered themselves

Close to me

The portion that helped me to realize

Those who had my best interest at heart

The portion that I can't relive,

But I pay homage to and have learned tremendously from

All the bad moments

The good moments

The moments that made me who I am today

I may not be who some want me to be

But I am who I was intended to be

The moments that positioned me

From sitting in the "scorner's seat and hurling the cynic's band"

To believing everyone has a chance at true happiness

The moments that restricted the gossiping tendencies of some

To plaque my heart and expel fallacies from my mouth

The moments that made me be still

Because peace is still

And like peace

We must all be still

If I could freeze time…

I would

Freeze it only for a second

Because my passion yearns to live unconstrained

Free to go as it pleases

Without the ill will of the world on its back

Riding it until any and all energy has been dissipated from its livelihood

Relinquishing its power and making it a

Freeze-framed part of what used to be

If I could freeze time..

I would

Freeze it only for a second

For a fraction of time

And let the world unwind

Wolf in Sheep's Clothing

He was a wolf in sheep's clothing

Telling lie after lie

Never making eye contact

Because those lies were in his eyes

He finally revealed himself

But only because he had been caught

A continuing relationship

Is something that was not sought

The part that really got me

Was his reason for telling me lies

"I'm a trained professional"

So the truth, I despise

"I actually didn't lie

I just didn't tell you the truth"

Then he questioned me

And asked me for the proof

The proof was in his words

In his thoughts

In his reply

That's why he's a wolf in sheep's clothing

Telling lie after lie

I Hear

I hear

Smooth

Soft

Drums

Playing

The sound is so inviting

So soothing for poetry writing

I analyze my situation

Discovering I'm pursuing

A life worth fulfilling

Through the beautiful melody

That is developing within me

I ask myself

Can this be?

Can my steps make music for thee?

Can my hands clap and produce a melody?

Can my feet produce a rhythm that amplifies me?

Only one way to see

Now listen

Listen

Listen to me

On your mark

Get set

Go

(Step)

Beautiful

Beautiful

Sound to my ears

The sound of stepping

That's what that is

Smooth

Soft Drums

Playing

A Street Called Daddy

Every night

He travels down the same dark path

Searching for a sunlit alley

Only to be thrown head first into the race that has rats dazed

I mean

He knows these streets better than the back of his own hand

That he can close his eyes and know that he can walk in darkness

But still be well protected

His father has a strange way of making him feel like the man

Making him put in overtime

For less than minimum wage

Making him slay his own brother

Because joy turned into rage

"Anger does not let him feel for a stranger"

For if he does

His character will be swallowed alive

Stepped on

With footprints left on his pride

He feels no less of a man

Than a father providing for his family

Who knows

He does the best he can

Daddy tells his children

Keep pushing hard

And stay up on your game

Because being a man

Is more than being a lame

He's so rigid

Making boys grow up before their time

Making them take the role of a man

But he fails to free their mind

He tells his children

I'm your daddy

And the street is the game

So, go strap up

Because it's time to rep

And maintain

Death!

Don't be scared

Because when it's your time

It's your time

Now soldier

Go throw on that track by Tupac

Ready to die

Do this for your family

You know I'll take care of you

But once life is gone

You know I'll have to replace you

You don't have to question

"How long will you mourn me?"

I'll tell you the truth

We'll mourn you for a second

And pour out some gin and juice

Then as the days go by

And even the years

We'll forget you

We won't even shed any tears

Your best friend will take your girl

Your child will be raised as his

He will speak not of you

Because yours is now his

I'm Addicted

I'm addicted

Emotionally attached to your personality

That pushes forward a confidence

Which displays so distinctively in your walk

I've tried to self-medicate

My emotional attachment by

Deleting the very means

That brings your existence into my mind

Let me say that again

I've tried to self-medicate

My emotional attachment by
Deleting the very means

That brings your existence into my mind

Scrolling through my cell phone and deleting

The communicative elements

That fed my addiction

Leaving no traces

Of the addictive substance

To be reintroduced into my body

That substance has the power of

Leaving my mind focused on an aspect of life

That seems so real

But really has been conjured up in my mind

The addiction has made it so hard for me to think clearly

Because I want to live carelessly

I want to love endlessly

I want to run jubilantly through a meadow

And release my energy into the environment

I want to release my inner self, which pushes through the pores of my skin

But is sometimes evaporated by the environment

As I reevaluate my addiction

I realize that my addiction is not because of you

My addiction is because of the passion that lives endlessly inside of me

And my power to put love into everything that I do

You have to know

I love me

So in turn

I love you

Caress Your Innermost Fears

I want to caress your innermost fears

While releasing burden from your body

Wrap my mind around your being

That you desperately try to hide

Embrace the warmth that dispenses

So flowingly through the pores of your epidermis

I want to sit on a couch with you

Divulging my womanly feelings

And intentions to you

I give you the power

For my heart knows when to be weak

When to skip a beat

When to not listen to my feet

For my feet tell me to run

Run past all the potential heartache and pain

That wants to cut off my blood flow

And circulation to the brain

My feet want to run freely

Run in the midst of like figures

And let the whole world see me

But until that day

I'll just sit here

Thinking of you

With your head on my shoulder

And caressing your fears

This is Temporary

This is temporary

My state of being is less than legendary

I plan to be here again

Never

Going to get my life together

For the better

It's not a choice

It's a must

I have more riding on this

Because the once me became us

I control my own destiny

If I take charge then the no's become yes to me

I must acknowledge that there are none to blame

I'm the queen of my own terrain

I have to admit

I thought I could make it

But now I know the outcome

I can't take it

Like I said this is temporary

My state of being will be legendary

I plan to be here again

Never

I have to get my life together

For the better

Again

This is temporary

Burden

I feel the burden of sorrow

Being placed around my ankles and wrists

That my breathing becomes shallow and rapid

My body tries to repair itself

From hyperventilating

However, I have become a prisoner within my own home

My temple is in disarray

Trying to defend itself from the sweet poison

That wallows out of the mouth of a venomous snake

That has good intentions, but fails repeatedly

I try to fight the captivity being placed on me

But I can't

The strange part is that there's familiarity in the disposition of my perpetrators

They seem of the loving sort

However they have became so engulfed with the poison within their body

That they would see it no other way

They would see no light

For the darkness continues to plague their eyes

Although their eyes are wide open

Although there's a cure to release the poison from their bodies

They take pride in watching others suffer at their own demise

I won't be a victim anymore

Because I have taken permanent refuge

Into a place that has the everlasting cure

I reside within me

Can I

Can I

Come into this room

As cool as I please?

Shining like the sunshine

Personality as cool as the breeze

Magnetic attraction

Draws inspiring souls

To the meeting places

Where some want to go

But not everyone knows

The words are spoken clearly

But the drive and determination have yet to surpass

The emotion is genuine

But will the feeling ever last?

I'm not in the business of pushing boulders

It's time to push yourself

And get the constraints up off your shoulders

I say

Can I come into this room

As cool as I please?

Being who I am

And shooting the breeze

I Miss You

I miss you

Three words that disrupt my mental functions

Of completing constant tasks

That use to be joyous

However have become more tedious than anything else

I sit staring at the wall

Obsessed with my own thoughts

That transition from you, work, and school

My world has started to slow down

At the train station of existence

Saying all aboard to my new conquests

And adieu to the dreams

That have made it to the mountaintop

A huge sigh of relief

Relinquishes itself from my body

Dissipating stress

Which looks for another host

To drain the life out of

I say

Demoralizing toxic

Be gone from my body

And let life return within me

Let the sun clear away the gray skies

And the moon cast light into darkness

Let my piercing ears

Hear not the easily digested words

Which focus so steadfastly on the disadvantage of others.

I miss you

Life

A place where dreams are not only figments of the imagination

But passion breeds those dreams into reality

A place where the race starts at birth

And ends at the departure of life

Where I can run freely among like incumbents

And more is expected, so more is achieved

I miss life

Where the Relay for Life

Is more of a team approach

And not an individualist sprint toward the finish line

I miss you

Because as the years progress

So does the distance and my connection with you

TV Show Poem

I was told

There's *Diff'rent Strokes*

For different folks

And it's *A Different World*

So, relax, relate, release

And ravish in *Boy Meets World*

The Facts of Life

Was to stay focused

While "moving on up"

And keep it *All in the Family*

or life will show you up

Like *Perfect Strangers* pushing along

Trying to show *Who's the Boss*

Realizing that *Family Matters*

Always is a must

Sanford and Son

Sold thrifty things

While asking

Are You Being Served?

While one's a loner

Two's a couple

and

Three's Company, too

Enjoy your years

As *Golden Girls*

And being the *Head of the Class*

While indulging in some Red Bull

To make the evening last

Stingy

He called me stingy

Because I held tight to my feelings

Like a virgin holds tight to her virginity

Not letting anyone in for the fear of betrayal

I provided no additional actions

That would make him think any differently about the statement

My mind then began separating that word

To bring clarity to my mind

Was I stingy?

Sting

A word that's less than stingy

And defines itself to mean a wound

Or some sort of puncture

Sing

A word minus the T

Which produces powerful vibrations

To bring forward feelings of like occurrences

In

Something that's trendy

A cutting-edge type of

Design or fashion

Stingy

A wound

Bringing forward feelings of like occurrences

That are trendy.

The Next Best Thing

Who am I you say?

I'm the next best thing

So, please make way

If you fail to see what's in me today

Someone will reveal it another day

If you fail to recognize me

You will recognize me soon

You just see

Go ahead

Make fun of me

Laugh at my ambition

You still shall see

Just know that I decided to keep pressing on

Because my target has been locked

And set for the moon

My dedication is out of this world

It has to be galactic

My measure of success

Is shown in my tactics

Maybe it's my super charge

Because like Beyonce

"I'm going to take it to the moon

Take it to the stars

How many people you know

Then took it this far?"

This far…

This far…

Remember

I'm the next best thing

So, please make way

Born to Be Deep

I was born to be deep

On some of my words

These people sleep

Born to take the path

Less traveled

Digesting me whole

Will leave your mind unraveled

You may have to take my words in doses

Because the truth isn't always honeysuckle and roses

Like En Vogue

You have to "free your mind"

Free the mental anguish

And release the bitterness from within

Your actions have been pleasant

But your thoughts have committed a sin

Your smile provides assurance

But your eyes have never learned to grin

You have to stop focusing on losing

And create a slogan that means to win

I was born

Born of the 12th day of May

Born to a one-parent home

But I made it anyway

Born with so much against me

That I must say

I was born

Born to be more than a mere uneducated woman

Who lets men walk up and down my spine

Because lack knowledge, did I

I was born from the womb

Mind still attached to the placenta of wisdom

Attracting like souls

And the inability to assume

I

Born in the times of foundation

Born to be me

In other words

I was born to be

Deep

Words; A Skilled Craft

Brain pickers

Thought trickers

Mind manipulators

Stealing ideas

And saving none for later

Idea takers

Sincere fakers

Switching from the Bulls to the Lakers

Speaking with enough poetic toxin

To turn a good girl bad

It's so sad

The words you chose to expel

Because a chance you never had

Poetic woes

Rhythmic flows

Disguising your gift

As a right on the spot

Love Jones

Deceptive truths

Labeled as aloof

But as I say

The pudding's

In the proof

Vice versa

Skilled tongues

Cow dung

Deceivers I'm among

Mind rippers

Strong tempers

Being in the company of

Skilled word pickers

From Pretty Women Wonder

From "pretty women wonder"

To "friends, fans, and artist must meet"

These are the lyrics

That my heroines speak

From Daniel's "knock, knock"

To the *Miseducation* of Lauryn Hill

From "living my life like it's golden"

Listen to all these lyrical skills

I listen so intently

Because these lyricists

Expose my mind to the multitude of mental satisfaction

That some have attempted to achieve

But failed considerably at what others perceive

If I could

I would wrap my body in the essence of Erykah's verbally influenced mind

Permanently implant the vocals of Lauryn Hill's song *When It Hurts So Bad* in my earlobe

Breathe in the passion of Maya's beautifully written poem about pretty women

I would answer Daniel's knock, knock

And tell him not to fear

Because truth and justice

Is finally here

Like Jill Scott

I have to live my life like it's golden

Because one life I'm permitted

And like in poker

I'm not folding

Thank you spoken truths

That flow so graciously

Out of the mouths of my teachers

Teach me

Teach me

To be me

Teach me

To live free

Teach to

To just be

Locked Gaze and Immovable Passion

I stand here

With a locked gaze and immovable passion

For I know

Success lies within my body

Pushing forward

Through my pores

And releasing an aroma

That intrigues others

Though I see

Not what they see

And smell

Not what they smell

I know the abstruse

Is often revealed

Perhaps my front-facing demeanor

Strong walking fever

Movement of my hands

Displays my passion and my plan

I see not what they see

Hear not what they hear

But feel emotion that has the power

To free burdened souls

And turn frowns

Upside down

My passion presses down on the paper

Forging out a carbon copy

Of feelings quarantined

These feelings

Are released with the right anecdote

A pen and paper

I stand here

Gaze locked

Passion Immovable

Ready to reveal my soul

Love Unreciprocated

I enter this unbound union

With an unconditional mindset

To love with all my heart

And leave no feelings unturned

I give my all

Only to have my ears overtaken

By the serpent's tongue

Of lies and dismay

The same tongue

Releases boisterous conditions

Which sound more like the rules of his love

I

A love guru

Take to those rules

Like a vegetarian takes to a medium well done steak

Not at all

My plate has no room

For things my body cannot hold

And lies are things

My body cannot hold

Love has been

Unreciprocated

Surface-Oriented People

Some people are surface-oriented people

Judging immediately

Without digging beneath the exterior

Of learned traits that have been classified as unacceptable

Their mouths release infectious diseases

That spread on the thoughts and mouths

Of others like them

The surface is the easy part

It provides no depth

No transparency

No recovery of a hidden treasure

No meaning behind the words

For the words are just words

Did they not hear the tone and emotion

Within those words?

Did they not see the passion

Dripping heavily from the fingers of the withered hands

And the cracked backs?

These people have taken on the responsibility of

Feeding on their own self-absurdness and insecurity

At the misfortunes of others

They are…

Surface-oriented people

The Type

You're the type that would date outside your race

He said

Verbally trying to abuse my character

Because he was that type

The type that sat inside coffee shops

Watching people of all walks of life go by

Unlike them

He sat in the shop

Giving his opinions

On matters which were not of his concern

My mind states so assertively

"To what do the world owe the pleasure

Of his loose lips and bitter tongue?"

Perhaps

Was it an unpleasant childhood

That made him an unpleasant man?

Was it the traits he had learned from his mother

Or even his father?

Was it the absence of a father figure in his life

Who was unable to teach him how to be a man?

Whatever it was

It was labeling him as a bitter individual

Who received pleasure

At the misfortunes of others

For I was nobody's type

I was undefined

Not labeling myself

Because I was just me

I was like FUBU

Living life

For me

By me

But that's something he probably could not understand

I'm nobody's type

Just a woman

My Life

Almost Raped

We Fall Down, But We Get Up!

Just Me!

What Will Be…

My Life

I sit here on a rainy September day, thinking and wondering about my life. Thinking about what it once was, what it is, and what it will be. My mind travels to two past experiences which molded me into the woman that I am today: the day I was almost raped and moments which made me appreciate life.

Almost Raped

Back in the day, my neighborhood was like a big family. We -protected each other from harm. We even uplifted each other to expect more than the hand we were dealt. It was like all the children in the neighborhood were birthed by the same mother and all the adults in the neighborhood were our aunts, uncles, grandmas, and grandpas. We were a family that prided ourselves on family and respect. People in our n-eighborhood, especially the children, were expected to act with the upmost respect. The fact of the matter was that if you did something bad in the community, your parents heard of the incident before you even reached home. Many times, you thought you were off scott free, well, until you reached home. That's just a brief example of who we were, what we expected, and how we protected each other.

I can remember a certain incident in my childhood that showed how very protective our community was of each other. The event -occurred right after my thirteenth birthday, so I had plenty of money in my pockets. I had awakened from one of my many well- appreciated naps and noticed I was missing something. The something was very special to me because being the age that I was, I did not come into contact with the object often. I was missing $10. If you were the same age as me with no job or viable income, $10 was a lot of money to be losing. I searched -inside my pants pocket, on the floor, and all over the house. I found nothing. It was like I was searching for a needle in a haystack with no precise location of where to search. After speaking with my mother and sister, I decided to check my sister's car. Maybe the money was there.

I went outside, playing the detective game and searching every inch of the landscape for anything green with a picture of Alexander Hamilton on it. Still nothing. As I approached my sister's car to continue using my searching tactics, as displayed on *Where in the World is Carmen Sandiego?* I heard a voice. The voice was a male voice stating "aye, wait." I looked in the direction of the voice, which was coming from an alley across from my home. The man's shirt was undone and he held up his pants, which seemed to drift further and further from his waist as he ran. Something told me that this man was not selling cookies and I needed to walk away from anything that he was selling. That walk turned into a run. I ran to my sister's car and frantically tried to open the car door. What was wrong with the door? Why did it not see how much I needed it to open right now? I needed to be safe because at this particular time, I did not feel safe. Right before he reached me, the door became ajar. I jumped into the car, slung the door shut, and locked it immediately.

This was definitely not my day. The man approached the car window and started banging on it. I cried immediately because I knew he did not have anything pleasant in store for me. He eased down his pants to display a portion of his manhood, which I had no business -seeing. Fear crept inside my spirit because I was trapped with only one way out: losing my virginity. I could not let him steal my womanhood. I just had to make it out alive. His pursuit to break the window did not work, so he retreated to a grassy area near my house. This was my o-pportunity to e-scape harm's way. I just knew that he was looking for something to break out the window with and I did not want to be there when he returned. I looked at the grassy area before making my next move. I did not see anything. I placed my sister's keys in my pocket with a plan to jump out of the car and run with all of my might. I darted out of the car and put my track and field experience to use. The only thing difference was, I did not stop running when I was out of sight.

On the next street, I found a man and a woman remodeling some apartments. I ran up to the door of the apartment and asked them to help me. I told them that some guy was trying to rape me and I needed help. The man and the woman stopped what they were doing immediately and came out of the apartment. At that time, my antagonist came running from around the corner. Seeing other people around me, he straightened up, tucked in his shirt, and walked up the street. The man I ran to for help worked quickly to gather some other men to go after my pe-rpetrator. The woman walked me home and told my mother and sisters what had happened. The police were called and came in five to ten minutes flat. Upon their arrival, the neighborhood men had caught the man who intended to inflict harm on me. It seemed as though the people of the neighborhood had taken matters into their own hands by conducting some of their own investigative methods.

Today, I look back at that day as the day I was almost raped. I just thank God that I was not raped and I am here to share my story.

We Fall Down, But We Get Up!

My lowest point in my life was when my doctor told me that there was a possibility that I had cancer. I could not believe it. How could I, a recent graduate of a small liberal arts college with so much to experience, have cancer? That question replayed over and over in my mind that I could not think or eat straight. What had I done or not done to acquire this? I did not smoke. Well, one puff or two puffs as a child does not constitute smoking, does it? I followed the healthy food guidelines, as set forth in the Health Promotion and Fitness course at my school. I admit that I had one or two days that I did not eat healthy, but I ate healthy for the most part, so that had to account for something.

Last, I did not sit outside on very hot or nice days and soak in the sun. I was familiar with the sun's strength and what it could do to my body.

Although I had scheduled a biopsy with a specialist to e-xamine my body, the news still took a toll on me. I became anti-social, did not sleep well, and became overly depressed. The very fact that I was -st-ruggling to make ends meet also wore on my spirit. Why? I questioned my creator, as if I was going through the denial stage of death and d-ying. Was I dying? I was only 24 years old; the age where it was ok for me to make mistakes because I had time to recover from them. My life was slipping right before my eyes and I could not pull the reigns and tell the driver to let me off this unexpected ride. Reality was more than I could handle. I usually loved the truth; however, this time I was hoping that the doctor had lied. I couldn't handle accepting his news as truth.

On the day of my surgery, my mother transported me to a -hospital on the west side. I was told that I would not be able to operate a motor vehicle after the operation and needed someone there for moral and physical support. My nurse connected me to an IV to help prepare me for surgery. I hoped that the IV would take away the hunger pains because I hadn't had anything to eat or drink within so many hours of my operation. After being connected to the IV for about an hour or two, I was whisked off to surgery with no clue in what to expect. My eyes were wide open; surveying the scene. The medical staff seemed very friendly, as they explained everything that was going to take place.

As my mind moved from the medical staff to my personal thoughts, I wondered what would happen if the anesthesia did not put me to sleep. I told myself, "They really think anesthesia is going to put me to sleep." Shortly after thinking about it, I felt a warm sensation in my right arm. The doctor spoke; however, his voice faded out, as did my vision. I woke up in a recovery room with a nurse checking my vital signs.

My movements were slow and relaxed. I felt like I was a drug addict; strung out and waiting for my next hit. Not only did I feel like an addict, I looked the part also.

The nurse led my mother to the recovery room to assist me with getting dressed. My mother looked at me and said, "my poor baby." Her eyes gazed over me somberly and she started helping her baby girl get dressed. The nurse gave my mother a prescription that needed to be filled, as she continued to help me get dressed.

After leaving the hospital, my mother took me to a grocery store near our home. She intended on filling the prescription she was given. I exited the car, walking as though I had just given birth a few hours ago. One of the employees asked my mother if I needed a wheelchair or some type of mobile device because it was apparent that I needed assistance. The lady returned with a wheelchair for me to sit down in. In any other instance, I would have tried to push through and make myself walk. However, I knew the employee was right. I sat in the wheelchair, while my mother filled the prescription. I was ready to get out of the chair and make my way to the car, but my plan did not go as planned. The e-mployee motioned someone to assist my mother with getting me to the car.

    I told myself to think more positively because I just had to get out of my depressive state. I did the best that I could, but the only thing that could get me out of that rut was the results. My primary care physician received the results in two to four weeks of the surgery. I met with him to discuss the results. My palms were shaky and I watched him as he carried a folder that had the power to change my life forever. He talked to me about my day and how was I doing. I was the type that wanted more of a direct answer and not a prolonged one. I was not disrespectful though, so I answered all of his questions. He finally revealed the results to me; I did not have cancer.

    I had fallen and could not get myself back up. There were so many things that happened in my life that I could not think straight. From that day on, I told myself "never again." Never will I let my -emotions and thoughts, get me down to the point where my existence is in question. Never will I be unhappy about things I cannot change. Never will I sit back and do nothing, as if I am helpless because I am not. I r-eclaimed my life and actually received more than I had started my -journey with. Now, It is your time to reclaim your life and say "never again."

Just Me

It is a warm October night. My thoughts rest on who I am today. I know I am just me. I wake up each morning, knowing who I am and what I must do. I must be who I was intended to be. Do what I was -intended to do. Meet who I was intended to meet. While this -information sounds vague to some, it provides all the knowledge I need to know, in order to keep being me.

Inspiration, for me, comes from others of like energy levels, who have the ability to reproduce the same vigor I have so willingly directed toward them. In my lifetime, I have only found a couple of individuals who have the ability to absorb my energy and redirect it toward me at the same level that it was given off. These individuals rejuvenate my -passion and give me strength to carry on. I am also inspired by dreams that seem so real that I just have to make them come true. I intuitively know that it is up to me to extract the needed information from my dream and take the necessary steps to reach for the stars. My challenge to everyone is to dig deep inside yourself to keep the courage, strength, dedication, -passion, action, and inspiration alive and pushing toward making a dream come true.

    Being me means having the ability to use negative and positive energy. Sometimes in life, people will act in a disrespectful manner to you, try to downplay your skills, and even use a technique of ignoring you; although you are the primary contact for the information they need. In this day and age, it is sad that people would act in this manner, but their behavior is something that you cannot change. What you can do is use their negativity and turn it into something powerful. Let not their ill will toward you deter you from being you and succeeding. Like the -saying goes "misery likes company." Be yourself and let misery stand on its own two feet and admire the view from afar. Using positive energy also makes it a win, win situation for you.

Some people choose to evaluate my life and thoughts and try to provide a summary of what is missing in my life. Me being who I am, I know that I miss not what others want me to because these are things that are important to them. While knowing these things are important to some, I encourage them to continue being them and let others find their own path to their wants, needs, and desires. It may be evident that these friends, family members, and acquaintances have my best interest at heart; however, I ultimately know that the decision is mine. So in your continuous journey, just be yourself and do what is best for you and not others. You have to live life for you.

It is still October. The weather is quite comfortable. While most would think October in Ohio would be cold and dreary, the weather has kept me guessing about the temperature and what to wear every day. The future is near, so my thoughts are on the future and what will be.

What will be...

I see the future, as if I am a fortune teller with premonition abilities. My continued writing with the ability to pull the reader into the subject matter will be unyielding and well developed. People will -experience the poetic person, who was once a silent individual that others thought to be aloof. My passion will continue to ignite the enthusiasm of others, who need a slight push to get them motivated. Life will show an abundance of experiences, opportunities, and development within and outside of me.

I see the future, not because I am one who possesses the -powerful ability to see life after now, but because I plan to write my own destiny. I plan to push myself and go for the goal. I plan to be all that I was -intended to be. My life was meant to be so much more than its current state. This is a feeling that sits in the back of my gut and pushes forward the more steps I take. I will not deny my body and spirit the right to experience life apart from this. I am motivated to make goals, amend -aspirations, and just experience the exhilarating feeling of completing tasks unbeknown to me.

I say this definitely

I am ready to take my place and go full throttle ahead!

Work Cited

Prophet (Poem)

    Shakespeare, W. (Playwright). (2003). Julius Caesar: Simon &

    Schuster. [Play]

The Womb: Life or Death (Poem)

    Philbin, J. and Hurdle, J. (Producers). (1955). The Honeymooners [TV Show]

    Badham, J. (Director). (1993). No Point of Return [Motion Picture].

If I Could Free Time... (Poem)

    Sirk, Douglas. (1959). Imitation of Life [Motion Picture]

    Foss, S. (Poet). (Year). House by the Side of the Road [Poem]

A Street Called Daddy (Poem)

    Shakur, T. (Musician) Against the World [Music]

    Shakur, T. (Musician) Ready to Die [Music]

Shakur, T. (Musician) How Thug Life [Music]

TV Show Poem (Poem)

Lear, N. and Yorkin, B. (Producers). (1978). Diff'rent Strokes [TV Series].

Cosby, B. (Creator). (1987). A Different World [TV Series]

Jacobs, M and Kelly, A. (Creators). (1993). Boy Meets World [TV Series]

Clair, D. and McMahon, M. (Creators). (1979). The Facts of Life [TV Series]

Nicholl, D., Ross, M., and West, B. (Creators). (1975). The Jeffersons [TV Series]

Lear, N. and Yorkin, B. (Creators). (1968). All in the Family [TV Series]

McRaven, D. (Creator). (1986). Perfect Strangers [TV Series]

Cohan, M. and Hunter, B. (1984). Who's the Boss [TV Series]

Bickley, W. and Warren, M. (Creators). (1989). Family Matters [TV Series]

Lear, N. (Producer). (1972). Sanford and Son [TV Series]

Croft, D. and Lloyd, J. (Creators). (1972). Are You Being Served? [TV Series]

Cooke, B., and Mortimer, J. (Creators). (1976). Three's Company [TV Series]

Harris, S. (Creator). (1985). The Golden Girls [TV Series]

Elias, M. and Eustis, R. (Creators). (1986). Head of the Class [TV Series]

The Next Best Thing (Poem)

West, K. (Contributor). (2011) Watch the Throne: Roc-A-Fella

Records. [Music]

From Pretty Women Wonder (Poem)

Angelou, M. (Poet). (1994). Phenomenal Woman: Random

House. [Book]

Badu, E. (Muscian/Poet). (2010). Friends, Fans, and A-rtist Must Meet. Def Poetry.

http://www.youtube.com/watch?v=mEXu6Um RPZc [Music]

Beaty, D. (Poet). (2010) Knock, Knock. Def Jam Poetry. http://www.youtube.com/watch?v=9eYH0AFx6yI [Poem]

Hill, L. (Musician/Poet). (1999). Miseducation of Lauryn Hill [Music]

Scott, J. (Musician/Poet). (2007). Golden. http://www.youtube.com/watch?v=4QCXr79Rkcw [Music]

Born to Be Deep (Poem)

En Vogue (Musicians). (2010). Free Your Mind. http://www.youtube.com/watch?v=i7iQbBbMAFE&ob=av2e [Music]

Words; A Skilled Craft (Poem)

Witcher, T. (Director). (1997). Love Jones [Motion Picture]

We Fall Down, But We Get Up (Essay)

McClurkin, D. (Musician). (2010). We Fall Down, But We Get Up.

http://www.youtube.com/watch?v=h3ewPHaPBfA [music]

My Poetic Soul Unleashed was brought to you by the creative talents of

Melica Niccole

Follow the author at MelicaNiccole.com,

Twitter.com/MelicaNiccole,

&

MelicaNiccolesRealmofCreativity.blogspot.com

Look for other titles by Melica

such as:

Dead Wrong

Poetic Outlets

Coming Soon:

All in Together Girls

Jacob

Hampton Publishing House, LLC can be contacted at

P.O. Box 1254* Union, NJ 07083* 614-25WRITE

www.ingramcontent.com/pod-product-compliance
Lightning Source LLC
Chambersburg PA
CBHW032018040426
42448CB00006B/650